100

Emma

from

Lil

5-84

"The pleasures of the table have ever held a distinguished rank amongst all those which man experiences in a state of society. It has been justly observed that they are the first of which we are susceptible, the last that we quit, and those that we can most frequently enjoy."

ESSAYS, MORAL, PHILOSOPHICAL, AND STOMACHICAL on the Important Science of Good-Living, by Launcelot Sturgeon, Esq., and dedicated to the Right Worshipful the Court of Aldermen of the City of London, 1822.

Other MINIMUM EFFORT MAXIMUM EFFECT COOK BOOKS published in Australia by The Terrace Times:

Paddington Edition
The Rocks Edition
Balmain Edition
Looking at Cooking
Melbourne Edition
City of Sydney Edition
Brisbane Edition

DEDICATED TO BRITISH AIRWAYS WHO, UNEXPECTEDLY AND DELIGHTFULLY, HELPED TO MAKE THIS BOOK POSSIBLE

First published in 1982
by William Collins Sons & Co. Ltd.
London . Glasgow . Sydney .
Auckland . Johannesburg

ISBN 0 00 411236 9
Printed in Hong Kong by the
South China Printing Co.

The London COOKBOOK

Drawings
by Ray Evans

Concept Text and Design
by Helen Arbib

INTRODUCTION

I must tell you, right away, that this is not a serious cook book for serious cooks. It is, instead, a light-hearted and illogical mixture of history, old buildings, cookery ideas, and minimum effort maximum effect recipes that allow us to lead our busy lives and still have a happy creative time in the kitchen.

It is the eighth book in the series. Something I could never have believed possible when I wrote and published my first one—for fun—and thought it was my last one. But, in fact, it is another first one... the first to be published by Williams Collins ... the first to be based in England. And in London, of all places!

London is my home town. Well, I'm lucky, I have two home towns and London is one of them. This is where I grew up and married, where I looked for bombs during the Blitz (though nobody told me what to do if I found one), where my eldest daughter was born, where many of my friends still live. This is where I have been flying back to ever since going to live in Sydney, Australia. But I never looked at London as closely, never enjoyed and appreciated it as much, as I have done while working on this book. What a wonderful city it is.

A special kind of book like this needs a special kind of artist. Someone like Ray Evans. Apart from his wide experience as artist and art teacher, his one-man shows in London and the provinces, his paintings in collections worldwide, he started his drawing career in an architect's office and one of his "main recreations" is good food. What could be more perfect than that?

The food in this book is English, much of it traditional, though the manner of preparing it is not. The recipes are all test-cooked of course. They are also test-eaten, which is interesting. How hard it has been to get family and friends to say what they really think, instead of making the usual polite and kind social noises.

I do hope you will read the Cookery Notes on Page 9 before you start to cook. And that the guidelines on Page 10 will prove helpful when metric conversion seems too hard to bear.

Helen Aubiel

St. Paul's Cathedral, on the cover, was designed by Sir Christopher Wren to replace the medieval St. Paul's destroyed by the Great Fire of London in 1666.
The sign on the title page hangs outside the Cheshire Cheese, said to be England's most famous pub. In Wine Office Court, off Fleet Street, it was patronised by such notables of their day as Dr. Johnson, Dickens and Mark Twain.

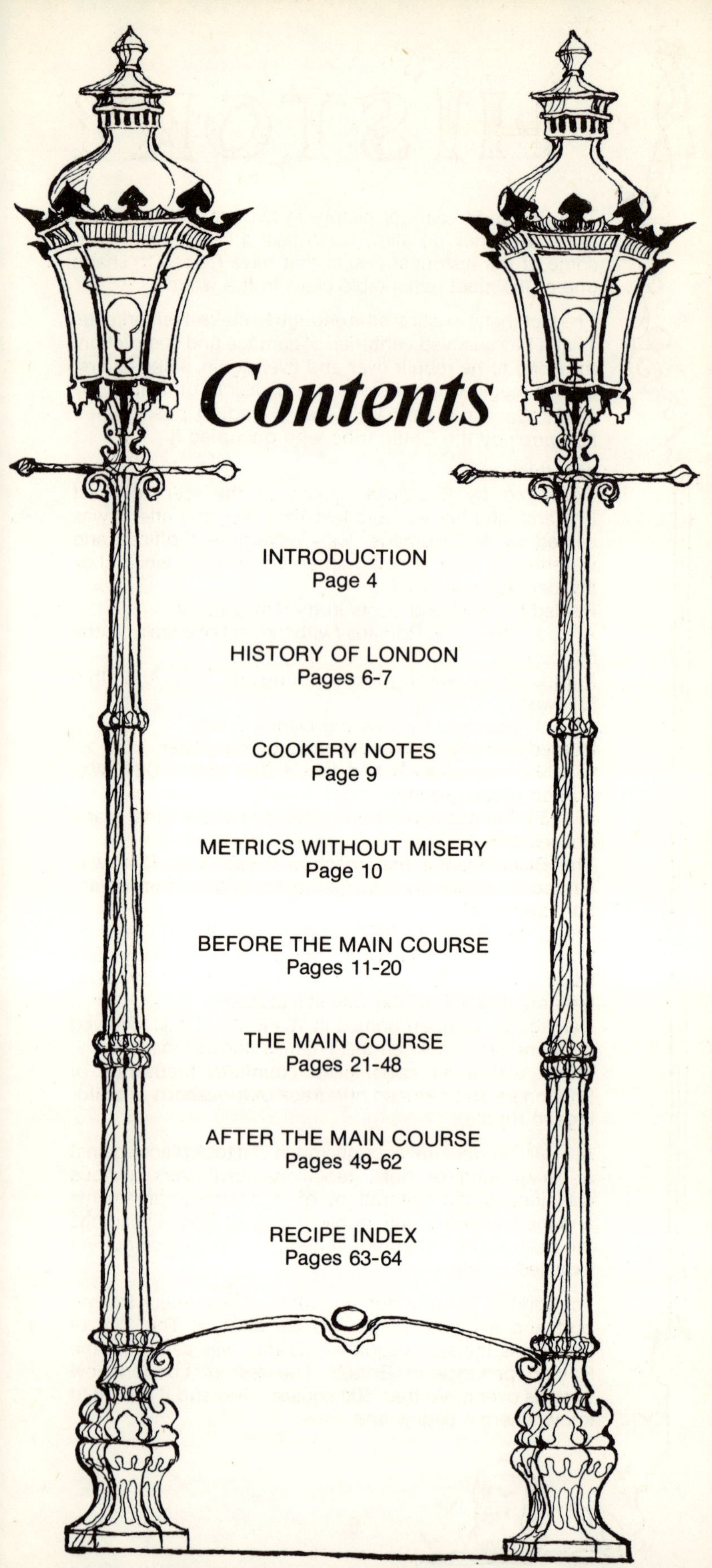

Contents

INTRODUCTION
Page 4

HISTORY OF LONDON
Pages 6-7

COOKERY NOTES
Page 9

METRICS WITHOUT MISERY
Page 10

BEFORE THE MAIN COURSE
Pages 11-20

THE MAIN COURSE
Pages 21-48

AFTER THE MAIN COURSE
Pages 49-62

RECIPE INDEX
Pages 63-64

HISTORY

Two thousand years of history in two small pages? Not really! But they do allow us to take a look, together, at some of the historical events that have helped to shape one of the most remarkable cities in the world.

The fact that it exists at all is enough to make it remarkable. That it has survived centuries of damage and destruction, the need to be rebuilt over and over again, since its first known beginnings—before the invasion of Britain by Julius Caesar in 55-54 BC—as a trading post named *Londinos* by the Celtic tribe who occupied it.

Just think of it.
Destroyed by Boadicea, queen of the Iceni of East England, and her warriors less than 20 years after it was settled by the Romans, with government offices and warehouses and a new name—*Londinium*, when they invaded again in AD 43.
Raided by Picts and Scots in the 4th century.
Abandoned by the Romans (with the rest of Britain) in the 5th century.
Plundered by warring tribes during the Dark Ages that followed.
All but destroyed by invading Danes in 839.
Burned and pillaged by Vikings a century later.
In 1096, "the greatest and fairest part of the City" was burned to the ground.
In 1136, fire destroyed London Bridge and a great many houses with it.
The Black Plague that reached England in 1346 was carried to London by wool merchants and half the population died of it.
The Great Plague of 1665 claimed over 68,000 lives.
The Great Fire of 1666, which began with a few flames in a baker's shop in Pudding Lane, burned for four days and left only one fifth of the City still standing.
Damage by German bombs in World War I was followed by more damage when the Thames flooded in 1927.
World War II air raids killed countless thousands of Londoners and reduced hundreds of thousands of buildings to rubble.

As if all this were not enough, much of it took place against a background of riots, rebellions, civil wars, various dissolutions and restorations of monastries, parliaments and the monarchy, with public hangings and beheadings the main source of entertainment for a populace not yet exposed to television.

Yet London became rich and famous as a major trading port and a centre of the world's finance. The City of London is the same square mile that was capital of the Roman province of Britain. The rest of London now sprawls over more than 600 square miles and it is hard to know where it begins and ends.

# of LONDON

Millions (billions? trillions?) of words must have been written about the history of London. It is an endlessly fascinating subject. But what I find most fascinating of all is that it is not just history confined within the pages of books. Londoners have kept it alive and well wherever we look. Not only in museums and galleries, in old buildings and monuments, but out in the streets as well.

It was in Drury Lane that Charles II fell in love with Nell Gwynne, and that Pepys first saw the crosses on the doors that signified the spread of bubonic plague. In a little house in Frith Street, Mahler composed his First Symphony. It was in the heart of the City that William the Conqueror was accepted as king in exchange for his guarantee of the laws and freedoms held under Edward the Confessor.

The Strand has been the main thoroughfare linking Westminster with the City since the 12th century. Fleet Street goes back to Roman times. Buried in the bed of the river Thames thousands of Roman coins and medallions have been found, 12 feet and more below the surface of today's London. And under the streets of London are the caves and cellars where Catholic priests said their forbidden Mass, when the monasteries were dissolved by Henry VIII, and the tunnels through which they escaped to the fields nearby.

The 17th century shop in Carey Street that sold silver mouse traps to elegant ladies, whose flour-powdered hair proved irresistible as a nesting place, no longer exists. But Carey Street does. And Piccadilly remains to remind us of the 17th century tailor who sold ruffs for doublets called piccadills and called his house Piccadilly Hall, a name that extended in time to the area around it.

There are, too, the ceremonies that keep the past alive. The annual presentation of a boar's head on a silver tray to the Lord Mayor by the Worshipful Company of Butchers, who expressed thanks in this way in the 12th century for a gift of land near the river Fleet where they could wash their meat. The celebration of the Spring Equinox by the Druid Order, near Tower Hill at Bryn Gwyn, an ancient burial ground. The admission ceremony of two new City Sheriffs each year, when nosegays are carried to record the outbreak of jail fever at Newgate Prison, killing Judges and Sheriffs, and the carrying of herbs at that time to ward off disease. An annual sculling race on the Thames with prizes from a legacy left by comedian Thomas Doggett in 1716.

Nobody in the world today can be certain where the future lies. But let's hope somebody will be writing the history of London 2,000 years from now!

BUCKINGHAM PALACE
was built as Buckingham House for the Duke of Buckingham in 1703, bought for George III in 1762, and remodelled by architect John Nash for George IV, when it was renamed Buckingham Palace. But he never lived there and it did not become the reigning monarch's permanent London address until Victoria's accession in 1837.
The interior, closed to sightseers, includes a Throne Room 66 feet long. The gardens cover 40 acres and contain a lake and one of the mulberry trees planted by James I to encourage England's silk industry.
The Palace is probably best known for the ceremonial Changing of the Guard that takes place here. When the royal standard is flying, it means the Queen is in residence.

COOKERY NOTES

Entertaining should be fun, a happy and relaxed way of letting people know we care about them.

When I started to entertain, I really did slave over the proverbial hot stove and, by the time my friends arrived, all I felt like saying to them was, "Here's the dinner. I hope you enjoy it. But I'm going to bed."

That was many years and many minimum effort maximum effect recipes ago. Before I discovered that taking short-cuts never does any harm to our reputations as gourmet cooks. But it does mean we can have a lot more time and energy to enjoy our own parties!

Short-cuts include:

* Accepting that dishes taste best when we use the best ingredients—fresh stock, freshly ground pepper, etc.—but that nothing disastrous will happen when we don't.
* Preparing extra quantities of chopped herbs, breadcrumbs, lemon juice, boiled rice, when there is time. Freezing them to use when there isn't.
* Cooking ahead, to avoid last minute panic. The recipes allow for this whenever possible.

Please note that:

* All recipes are planned for 6-8 people.
* All spoon measurements are level.
* Plain flour is used unless otherwise specified.
* Recipes are flexible enough to allow for variation in tin sizes, not just from one town or country to another, but from one shop to another. A little more or less of any tinned ingredient won't matter.
* Culinary terms vary. Names most commonly used in England are listed first, e.g. peppers/ capsicums.
* And products vary. Only single and double cream, for pouring and whipping, are specified from the enormous range available in England, as some countries use just one cream for everything.

Finally, if we are to streamline our cooking, it is only logical that we should streamline our attitude to kitchen metrics as well. After all, nobody cares if our 'medium onion' is not the same weight as the 'medium onion' in a recipe and it is obviously equally unnecessary to worry about the small differences that occur with metric conversion.

An ounce equals 28.35 grams, but no cook can be expected to cope with multiples of this—and stay sane! So recipes allow 30 grams to the ounce and give both metric and imperial measures ... which must never be mixed. I have also worked out the guidelines on the following page to ensure relaxed cooks and successful cooking, though they make no sense mathematically.

METRICS WITHOUT MISERY

Level Teaspoons	Level Tablespoons	Grams (g)	Milli-litres (ml)	Ounces (oz)
1=		5	5	
3=	1	15	15	
6=	2	30	30	1

In UK, USA, Canada, South Africa, New Zealand.

But in Australia:

Level Teaspoons	Level Tablespoons	Grams (g)	Milli-litres (ml)	Ounces (oz)
4=	1	20	20	
6=	1½	30	30	1

So ... teaspoons are not converted to tablespoons in the recipes, to allow everyone to do their own sums.

Grams	Kilograms (kg)	Ounces	Pounds (lbs)
30=		1	
60=		2	
90=		3	
110=		4	¼
125=		4½	
225=		8	½
350=		12	¾
450=		16	1
500=	0.5	18	
1000=	1	36	2¼

Milli-litres	Litres	Fluid Ounces	Imperial Pints	USA Pints
30-125=		1-4½	as grams and ounces	
225=		8		½
300=		10	½	
450=		16		1
600=		20	1	
1000=	1	35	1¾	2¼

Milli-litres	Metric Cups	Fluid Ounces	Imperial Cups	USA Cups
225=		8	1	1
250=	1	9		

Liquids only. Solids vary according to ingredients.

Oven Conversions—Celsius and Fahrenheit

140C=275F 150C=300F 170C=325F 180C=350F

190C=375F 200C=400F 220C=425F 230C=450F

Kitchen Utensils—Centimetres and Inches

2.5cm = 1 in 20cm = 8 in 25cm = 10 in 30cm = 12in

Before the Main Course

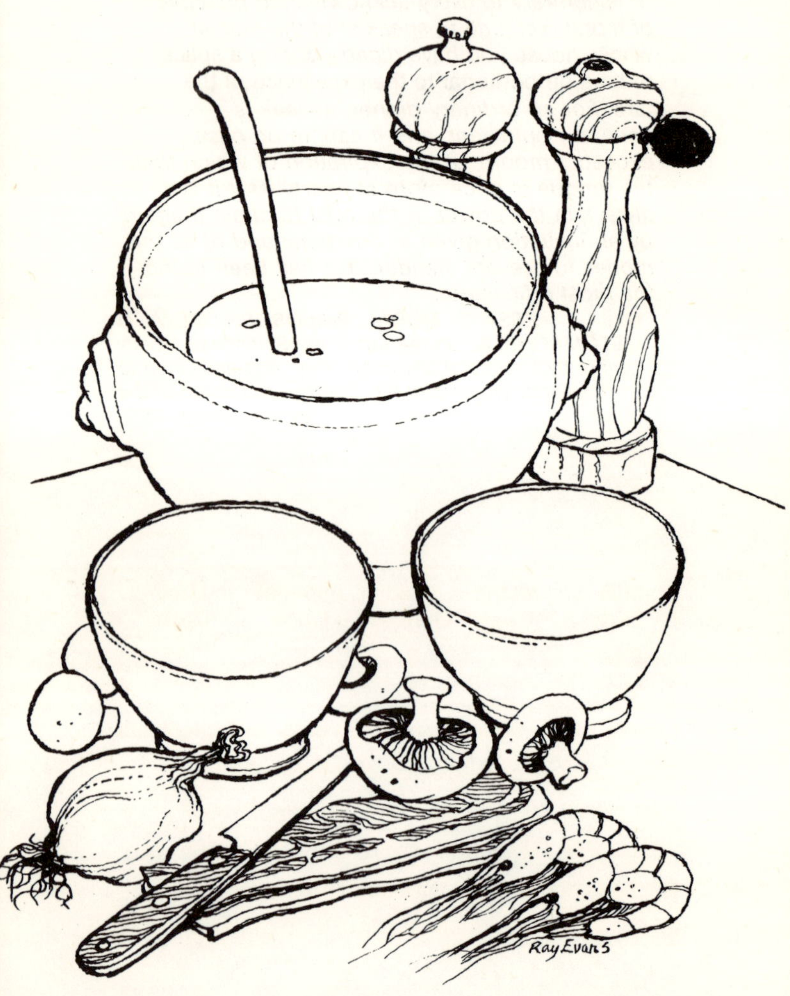

"It is contrary to every acknowledged principle of moral rectitude to speak ill of the man at whose house you have dined—during a space of time proportional to the excellence of the fare. *For an ordinary dinner, a week is generally sufficient; and it can, in no case, exceed a month; at the expiration of which time, the tongue is once more at liberty. But it is always in the power of the host to chain it again by an invitation given in due time: and of all the modes to prevent slander, this has been found the most efficacious."*

ESSAYS, MORAL, PHILOSOPHICAL, AND STOMACHICAL on the Important Science of Good-Living, by Launcelot Sturgeon, Esq., and dedicated to the Right Worshipful the Court of Aldermen of the City of London, 1822.

Whets

Whets (as distinct from political wets) was the 18th century name for the delightful mouthfuls that whetted the appetite for the meal to follow.

Today we call them appetisers but many of us, when we are busy, fall into the trap of serving a few pretzels and peanuts instead. Which is a pity. If we are going to serve a delicious dinner, surely we ought to start the evening equally deliciously.

Prawns in Bacon can be prepared ahead, cooked quickly in the oven when guests arrive.

Allowing 1 per person, peel and devein
- 6-8 very large prawns, that will cut into 3 pieces approx. 3cm (1¼") each ... if shorter prawns are bought, buy enough to cut into right number of pieces.

Cut prawns. Remove rind and cut into 3 pieces
- 6-8 rashers smoked bacon

Roll prawn pieces in bacon. Fix with toothpicks. When required, place join-side down on baking tray. Cook 10 minutes in 200C/400F oven. Serve immediately, with cocktail napkins.

Cheddar Cheese Dip should be served with chilled raw vegetable pieces ... cucumber and carrot sticks, button mushrooms, cauliflower florets, etc. etc.

Combine in bowl and chill at least 3 hours
- 400g (14oz) plain yoghurt
- 250g (9oz) well matured Cheddar cheese, grated
- 2 teaspoons prepared English mustard
- 8 teaspoons finely chopped parsley
- 8 teaspoons finely chopped chives
- 1 teaspoon each paprika and lemon juice
- ⅛ teaspoon white pepper

*It can also be folded into small chilled inner lettuce leaves, and eaten with thin slices of buttered toast.

"Eating is heaven!"

CONFUCIUS, 551-479 B.C.

ST. BARTHOLOMEW-THE-GREAT, SMITHFIELD

This splendid Norman Priory Church, the oldest church in London except for the chapel in the Tower, was founded in 1123 by Rahere, a courtier of Henry I. Despite considerable destruction during the Reformation, the choir he built still stands, as does the watching window added by its last prior. The Lady Chapel was once used as a printing office, notable for the fact that American statesman and philosopher Benjamin Franklin worked there.

Above the gateway to the church is a house with a half-timbered facade that dates back to the time of Elizabeth I. It was discovered during World War I, when a German bomb loosened the tiles that had concealed it. In the little graveyard, each Good Friday after the 11am service, hot cross buns and coins are placed on tombstones as a gift for poor widows, a custom dating back to 1686.

Soups

Of course there are many happy ways to start a meal but soups have always been my favourite. Hearty warming soups in winter. Elegant chilled soups in summer. And those in between when it ought to be summer—and isn't.

Mulligatawny Soup. A 'pepperwater' brought back to England by the British in India during the 18th century.

Brown lightly in frying-pan
 4 chicken thighs, in
 90g (3oz) unsalted butter or margarine
Transfer to large saucepan. Brown in remaining fat, adding more if necessary
 2 each carrots, onions, celery stalks, sliced
Add to chicken. Crush in frying-pan
 6 cloves and 6 peppercorns
Add and stir until dark brown
 8 teaspoons flour, mixed with
 3-4 teaspoons hot curry powder to taste
Add to chicken with
 1 large cooking apple, peeled, cored and chopped
 4 teaspoons desiccated coconut
 1¾ litres (3 pints) chicken stock, or water with 3 10g (⅓oz) dissolved stock cubes
Simmer, covered, about 1½ hours. Remove chicken. Chop best pieces and return to soup. When required, reheat with
 juice 1 large lemon
Serve with
 4 teaspoons boiled rice in each bowl
 mango chutney on the side.

"In London, man rubs out, elsewhere he rusts out. No doubt the mental stimulus of London staves off much disease, for idle men eat themselves to death and worry themselves to death; but in city life neither gluttony nor worry has a chance."
LONDON CHARACTERS, HENRY MAYHEW, 1881.

Watercress, finely chopped and pushed into the ears, was once regarded as a fool-proof cure for *toothache*!

Creamy Chilled Mushroom Soup. To be made and served the same day.

Wash, dry, and chop roughly
  500g (18oz) large mushrooms
Purée in blender or processor with
  250ml (9 fluid oz) water
In large saucepan cook, stirring, on low heat
  60g (2oz) butter or margarine, melted
  4 teaspoons flour
When bubbly, stir in slowly
  mushroom purée
  1 litre (1¾ pints) chicken stock, or water with
    3 10g (⅓oz) dissolved stock cubes
Bring to boil, stirring constantly. Reduce heat.
Simmer 5 minutes. Cool and stir in
  225ml (8 fluid oz) single cream from 300ml
    (10 fluid oz) carton
  salt and pepper to taste
  ⅛ metric (tea) cup chopped parsley
Cover and chill well. Chill reserved cream and, before serving, swirl it through soup with fork for colour contrast.

Stilton Soup. Very luxurious.

Combine in large saucepan over low heat
  110g (4oz) flour, with
  110g (4oz) melted butter or margarine
Remove from heat. Stir in gradually
  900ml (1½ pints) milk
  900ml (1½ pints) chicken stock, or water with
    2 10g (⅓oz) dissolved stock cubes
Return to heat and bring to boil, stirring.
Immediately it boils, add
  300g (10oz) Stilton cheese, crumbled
  2 teaspoons dried onion flakes
  ½ teaspoon each salt and paprika
Simmer gently 5 minutes. Just before serving, stir in
  225ml (8 fluid oz) single cream
Reheat without boiling. Garnish with
  a light sprinkle paprika
*Quantities are on the generous side, as portions should be small because soup is so rich. But it is risky not to allow for second serves because it's so good.

"It is by far too common a practice to offer guests a variety of wines with high-sounding names which really only disguise liquid poison. Nothing can exceed the treachery of asking people to dinner under the guise of friendship, and then giving them either to eat or to drink of that which may be injurious to health."
LITTLE DINNERS, MARY HOOPER, 1874.

In Shakespeare's day, before Mr. Colman made mustard a household word, the seeds were crushed between cannon balls and added to sauces. In the 18th century a Mrs. Clements made her fortune with the first fine powder to be mixed with water; her most famous customer George I, the Georgie Porgie of the nursery rhyme.

Baked Soup from an old cook book. Filling and trouble-free.

A day or 6-7 hours ahead, wash in cold water
1 metric (tea) cup green split peas
Remove any that are badly discoloured or that float. Drain. Soak 3 hours in large pan in
1 metric (tea) cup warm water
Then add, without changing water
450g (1lb) gravy beef, chopped small
1 rindless bacon rasher, chopped small
250g (9oz) onions, sliced
250g (9oz) carrots, sliced
250g (9oz) celery, sliced
3 teaspoons salt and ¼ teaspoon pepper
Add cold water (the recipe specified spring water!) to cover meat and vegetables. Cook, tightly covered, in 180C/350F oven 3 hours or until reduced by about a third.
Reheat when required.

A Most Unusual Chilled Yoghurt Soup. It can be prepared the previous day.

Soak 10 minutes.
110g (4oz) seeded raisins, in
450ml (15 fluid oz) water
Drain raisins over large bowl. Put on one side.
Stir into raisin water
450g (1lb) plain yoghurt, followed by
250ml (9 fluid oz) single cream
110g (4oz) peeled, seeded, finely chopped cucumber
110g (4oz) chopped walnuts
2 hard-boiled eggs, finely chopped
30g (1oz) spring onions/shallots, finely chopped
drained raisins
2 teaspoons salt
½ teaspoon white pepper
Chill, covered, at least 3 hours.
Serve small portions garnished with finely chopped parsley and dill leaves.

Pork crackling, toughened in boiling fat, was shaped into shields by the Normans to use in battle against the arrows and axes of their enemies.

Superb Devonshire Cauliflower Soup.

Place in large saucepan
1 medium firm white cauliflower, cut into small florets, with
600ml (1 pint) boiling water
Cover. Boil 10 minutes. Drain and reserve liquid.
In same saucepan, sauté until soft and golden
1 large onion, finely chopped, in
60g (2oz) butter or margarine
Blend in
8 teaspoons flour, followed by
750ml (1¼ pints) chicken stock, or water with 10g (⅓oz) dissolved stock cube
Cook and stir over medium heat until sauce is creamy. Add
250ml (9 fluid oz) each cauliflower liquid, milk, and single cream
¾ teaspoon salt
½ teaspoon Worcestershire sauce
Add cauliflower and bring to boil, stirring.
Remove from heat and stir in
250g (9oz) mature Cheddar cheese, grated
Serve sprinkled with
chopped parsley.

Cock-a-Leekie, an 18th century Scottish soup still popular today. Prunes add colour and a distinctive touch of sweetness.

Combine in large saucepan
1kg (2¼lbs) chicken pieces
450g (1lb) veal knuckle, sliced by butcher
cold water to cover
Bring to boil. Remove any scum.
Cover and boil gently about 1½ hours.
While soup cooks, trim coarse ends from
6 medium or 4 large leeks
Halve lengthwise. Wash well. Cut into 2½cm (1″) pieces. Also soak in a little hot water
110g (4oz) stoned prunes
When chicken is tender, remove it and veal.
Add leeks and prunes with
1 metric (tea) cup freshly chopped parsley
Boil gently 8-10 minutes until leeks are cooked.
Add best pieces of chicken, chopped.
Reheat when required. Season to taste and serve with or without prunes.

In Scotland, in the 18th century, cock-fights were commonly held in parish schools to celebrate the Festival of Lent. Not surprisingly, cock-a-leekie was a popular supper for Fastern's E'en, which precedes the first day of Lent; it was made with the fugie ... the defeated bird.

Entrées

Although the French word *entrée* means 'beginning,' it has never related to the beginning of a French meal; rather strange for a nation noted for its logic. In a full menu, it is the third course that follows the fish and precedes the meat.

For most of us who entertain at home, with rather less ambitious menus, it does precede the meat—or whatever else is served in its place. But, without all the other courses, it *becomes* the beginning of the meal.

Hot Fish Mousse.

In blender or processor, chop
4 teaspoons parsley
Add, and purée in bursts, scraping down sides with a spatula until smooth
225g (8oz) fillets cod or other firm white fish, boned and skinned
Add and combine briefly
1 egg
150ml (5 fluid oz) double cream
1 teaspoon salt
⅛ teaspoon black pepper
Pour into greased soufflé dish or 6-8 individual ramekins. Sprinkle with
grated Parmesan cheese
Stand in baking tin with hot water ½ way up sides. Bake in 170C/325F oven 30 minutes for small dishes, 40 minutes for large one.

Cool Minted Pears for summertime.

Allowing 2 per person, drain on paper towelling
12-16 tinned pear halves
Arrange core-side up on serving dish, with small sliced cut from base so they sit flat.
Top with
300g (10oz) sour cream, blended with
2 teaspoons white vinegar
½ teaspoon salt
⅛ teaspoon white pepper
4 teaspoons caster sugar
4 teaspoons fresh mint, finely chopped
Chill well. Serve each half garnished with
a very light sprinkle slivered almonds
a tiny sprig of mint.

Spinach and Ricotta Pie. Almost as good cold as it is hot, it will do double duty as entrée or light main dish.

Prepare lining and top for 25cm (10″) pie dish, as package instructions, with
ready-made puff pastry
Line dish. Mix well together in bowl
250g (9oz) chopped cooked spinach, or uncooked frozen spinach weighed after thawing and draining
225g (8oz) ricotta cheese
2 eggs, lightly beaten
125ml (4½ liquid oz) milk
½ teaspoon each salt and Worcestershire sauce
Fill pie shell. Sprinkle with
90g (3oz) Cheddar cheese, grated
Cover with pastry top. Press edges together, with fork for decorative effect. Cut 5 slits in centre for steam to escape. Glaze with
milk or beaten egg yolk
Decorate if you wish with
cut-out pastry leaves
4 teaspoons sesame seeds
Cook in hot 230C/450F oven ¾ hour or until golden brown.

Remarkable Wholemeal Bread. Making bread has a special magic all its own, so it's sad that it can also be intimidating. But not with this remarkable recipe: so easy because the dough rises in the loaf tin.

Just mix together
1 teaspoon dried yeast
1 teaspoon brown sugar
300ml (10 fluid oz) warm water
Leave in warm place to froth up, while mixing in a large bowl
450g (1lb) wholemeal flour
1 teaspoon salt—sea salt, if available
Add yeast mixture gradually and mix by hand to make a damp non-sticky dough, adding a little more flour or water if necessary.
Put dough into well-greased loaf tin. Cover with clean cloth. Place in oven preheated to its lowest setting. Leave 30 minutes to rise.
Remove cloth. Turn up oven to 200C/400F and cook bread 1 hour or until skewer comes out clean. Turn out and cool.

*A delicious dense-textured, heavy loaf, it should be thinly sliced with a very sharp knife.

The Main Course

On Modern Manners—Carving.
"If an accident should happen, make no excuses, for they are only an acknowledgement of awkwardness. We remember to have seen a man of high fashion deposit a turkey in this way in the lap of a lady; but, with admirable composure, and without offering the slightest apology, he finished a story he was telling at the same time, and then, quietly turning to her, merely said—'Madam, I'll thank you for that turkey.' "

ESSAYS, MORAL, PHILOSOPHICAL, AND STOMACHICAL on the Important Science of Good-Living, by Launcelot Sturgeon, Esq., and dedicated to the Right Worshipful the Court of Aldermen of the City of London, 1822.

Fish and Poultry

Simple Spicy Special Kedgeree. Translated from the Hindu *khichri*, kedgeree dates back to the days of the British Raj in India, adapted for English breakfasts and suppers without the spices that must have characterised it originally. This adaptation of the adaptation makes an excellent dinner dish.

Fish, eggs and rice can be cooked a day ahead and refrigerated; combined with sauce and heated just before serving.

In large shallow pan, pour boiling water over
  1¾kg (4lbs) smoked haddock
Simmer gently 10 minutes. Drain, discard skin and bones, flake finely. Hard-boil and slice
  4-5 eggs
Boil as packet instructions
  400g (14oz) long grain rice
For sauce, combine and heat in large saucepan
  425g (15oz) tin cream of celery soup
  ½ soup tin milk and single cream, combined
  1-2 teaspoons curry powder
  1 teaspoon ground cumin
  ½ teaspoon ground chillies
  ½ metric (tea) cup freshly chopped parsley
Stir in haddock and rice. When hot and just before serving, add sliced eggs.
*Alternatively, stir haddock, rice and eggs into sauce, and cook in casserole, covered, in 150C/300F oven 20 minutes or until hot.

Savoury Salmon Custard. "Sheer bliss," said the friend who gave it to me, but nobody wanted to try it until I called it a soufflé.

Drain and remove skin and bones from
  650g (1lb 7oz) tinned red salmon
Mash lightly with fork. Combine in bowl with
  5 eggs, lightly beaten
  410g (14½oz) tin evaporated milk
  ¼ teaspoon salt and ½ teaspoon paprika
  a light sprinkle of pepper
Pour into greased soufflé or casserole dish. Stand in baking tin in hot water. Cook in 180C/350F oven 45-55 minutes or until firm.
Garnish with
  chopped chives or parsley
Serve hot or cold.

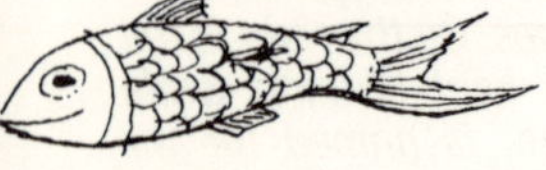

THE HOUSES OF PARLIAMENT
were rebuilt after most of the Old Palace of Westminster, home of succeeding sovereigns from the 11th to the 16th centuries and seat of government from 1547, was destroyed by fire in 1834. They are also known as the New Palace of Westminster.
On the left is the tallest square tower in the world, Victoria Tower, which is occupied by the House of Lords where the Queen and her Consort, the Duke of Edinburgh, have their thrones. On the right is the 320 feet high Clock Tower, where a light is kept burning while Parliament is sitting. Its famous bell, Big Ben, *is named for Sir Benjamin Hall who was First Commissioner of Works when it was cast.*

The House of Commons, in turn, was virtually destroyed by fire during air raids in 1941, and has been rebuilt. It originally met in St. Stephen's Hall, which has four brass rosettes set into the floor where Charles I was forbidden by the Speaker to enter and arrest five of its members. No sovereign was admitted to the House of Commons from that time until George VI visited the new chamber, a period of some 300 years.

Westminster Hall was originally built in 1097 by William II, had its magnificent timber roof added about 1394 by Richard II, but this did not prevent his being deposed in the Hall in 1399. It was here that Charles I was condemned to death. It was in the Old Palace Yard that Sir Walter Raleigh was beheaded.

Rhubarb appeared in England as early as the 16th century, but only as a decorative plant grown around ponds.

Fish with Mayonnaise and Bread Cubes may (does!) sound decidedly peculiar, but the end result is succulent and decorative.

For 6-8, arrange in layers in well-greased shallow oblong oven-to-table dish
  1-1⅓kg (2¼-3lbs) fillets of any firm white fleshy fish, skinned and bonned
Gently stir
  6 thick slices bread, with crusts removed and cut into small cubes, into
  75-90g (2½-3oz) hot melted butter or margarine, enough to thoroughly coat them
Reserve cubes. Combine in bowl or jug
  1 cup egg mayonnaise
  1 egg yolk, lightly beaten
  2 teaspoons tomato sauce
  ¼ teaspoon mustard powder
  1 clove garlic, crushed or finely chopped
  4-5 drops Worcestershire sauce
Spread evenly over fish. Top evenly with bread cubes. Cook, uncovered, in 180C/350F oven 20-30 minutes, or until fish flakes when tested with fork (it must not overcook) and cubes have browned. Serve immediately.

Sweet and Sour Fish Fillets with Ginger.

For 6-8, cut into serving-size pieces
  1-1⅓kg (2¼-3lbs) cod or fresh haddock fillets, with bones and skin removed
Fry on medium-high heat in shallow pan in
  60-90g (2-3oz) mixed oil and butter, or oil and margarine
When lightly coloured, remove from pan.
Sauté until soft in remaining fat
  6-8 shallots/spring onions, chopped
Remove from heat. Add fish. Combine in bowl
  45g (1½oz) fresh ginger, finely chopped
  110ml (4 fluid oz) vinegar
  110ml (4 fluid oz) soy sauce
  60g (2oz) sugar
  6 teaspoons oil
Pour over fish. Simmer, covered, 4-5 minutes. Turn fish. Taste sauce. Add a little sugar if required. Cover and simmer 4-5 minutes more or until fish flakes when tested with fork.
Serve hot, garnished with
  freshly chopped chives or parsley.

"The aborigines of Britain objected to eat fish, whilst they were not unwilling to eat seals and porpoises."
FOODS, EDWARD SMITH, 1873.

STAPLE INN, HIGH HOLBORN
Built in 1586, its gabled and timbered facade is a rare example of a genuine Tudor building of Shakespeare's day. A hostel first, it was an Inn of Chancery from Henry V's reign until 1884, one of several small inns used as legal educational establishments.

Chicken with Seafood Sauce. I am always surprised when friends are surprised by this twosome. They really are wonderful together.

Combine in large pan, allowing 1 per person
- 6-8 large chicken breast halves
- 1 medium onion, chopped
- 1 medium unpeeled carrot, chopped
- 1 stalk celery and leaves, chopped
- 6 peppercorns and 1 bay leaf
- 10g (⅓oz) chicken stock cube, dissolved in 450ml (15 fluid oz) hot water
- 150ml (5 fluid oz) white wine
- 6 teaspoons lemon juice
- 1½ teaspoons salt

Bring to boil. Reduce heat, cover, and boil gently (why don't they make saucepan lids with little windows?) 20-30 minutes, just until chicken is tender. Cool in pan. Place chicken pieces side by side in shallow oven dish. Strain broth into separate container for sauce.
If cooked ahead, cover and refrigerate.

When required, heat broth with
- 225g (8oz) small prawns or shrimps (half this quantity if peeled), chopped
- 175g (6oz) fresh or tinned crabmeat, flaked
- 1 metric (tea) cup freshly chopped parsley
- salt and white pepper if required

Add for thickening, as necessary
- 4-6 teaspoons cornflour, dissolved in equal quantity water

Stir over heat until blended. Pour over chicken. Cover and cook in 170C/325F oven 20-30 minutes, only until chicken is heated through.

Chicken Baked with a Curry Sauce.

Allowing 2 pieces per person, shake together in plastic bag
 6-8 each chicken thighs and legs, in
 60g (2oz) flour, seasoned with
 1½ teaspoons salt
 2 teaspoons ground ginger
Discarding excesss flour, roll pieces in
 60g (2oz) melted butter or margarine
Stand on paper towelling to drain off excess fat. Arrange in baking tin. Cook 30 minutes in 200C/400F oven, while making sauce.

For sauce, remove rind and chop finely
 225g (8oz) lean bacon
Sauté in saucepan 2-3 minutes. Drain off fat and stir in
 425g (15oz) tin beef consommé
 1 medium onion, finely chopped
 6 teaspoons apple sauce
 6 teaspoons flour
 6 teaspoons fruit chutney
 6 teaspoons lemon juice
 6 teaspoons desiccated coconut
 2-3 teaspoons hot curry powder to taste
 2-3 teaspoons sugar to taste
Bring to boil, stirring. Reduce heat. Simmer 10 minutes, stirring occasionally. Spoon over chicken. Return to oven 30 minutes or until tender.

Chicken Ring. Quick and easy way to transform leftover chicken or a ready-cooked bird.

Beat lightly in mixing bowl
 2 eggs, or 3 egg yolks
Heat and pour onto eggs, stirring constantly
 250ml (9 fluid oz) each milk and single cream
Add and mix well
 450g (1lb) skinless cooked chicken, diced
  (weight can be made up with packet ham)
 60g (2oz) soft white breadcrumbs
 small green pepper/capsicum, finely chopped
 long inner stalk celery, finely chopped
 6 teaspoons lemon juice
 1 teaspoon Worcestershire sauce
 1 teaspoon salt and ¼ teaspoon paprika
Put into well greased 6-7 cup ring mould. Cook in 150C/300F oven 45 minutes or until knife comes out clean—do not overbake.
Let stand 10 minutes before unmoulding.
Serve with Garlic Sauce (Page 47) and well drained chopped spinach piled in centre.

THE TOWER OF LONDON AND TOWER BRIDGE
Variously said to have been founded by Julius Caesar, and begun by William the Conqueror as a fortress against attacks that never came (history is like that), the Tower stands on almost 18 acres of land at Tower Hill, surrounded by a deep moat that is now a public garden. It is guarded by Yeoman Warders, best known as Beefeaters (supposedly named for meat rations allocated to them in ancient times), who still wear Tudor costume.
The Tower was also a palace until this was destroyed by Cromwell. And a prison. A fearsome place stained with the blood of some of history's most famous characters, among them Ann Boleyn, one of Henry VIII's discarded Queens, and Sir Thomas More, who died protesting he was "the King's good servant but God's first" and whose head was displayed to the populace, spiked on London Bridge. Here, in the dungeons, Guy Fawkes and his fellow conspirators were among those chained and tortured.

Tower Bridge, which spans the river Thames below the Tower, is 940 feet long and 60 feet wide, somewhat different from the first narrow wooden bridge that was built by the Romans and destroyed by the Danes.

Pheasant Pie. A freshly-shot pheasant used to be carried proudly home and suspended from one of its long tail feathers. When it fell from the feather, it was "ripe for the spit". Today, game birds usually come bred for the table and ready to cook; this recipe is ideal for older frozen birds. Without pastry, it is served as a casserole.

Allow to thaw completely
  3 frozen pheasants, total weight approx. 2¾kg (6lbs)
At the same time, to avoid an overcooked or soggy crust, prepare as packet instructions
  ready-made puff pastry
to fit top of large (approx. 5½ litre/5 quart) flameproof oven dish. Cook on greased baking tray in 230C/450F oven until golden.

If using pheasants' heads, feet and giblets for stock (rather than water and cube), cover with water and boil gently while cutting birds into serving-size pieces.
In the large flameproof dish, melt
  30g (1oz) unsalted butter or margarine
Stir in over medium heat
  350g (12oz) streaky bacon, rind removed and finely chopped, followed by
  2 medium onions, sliced
  3-4 medium carrots, sliced
When onions are soft but not brown, stir in
  250ml (9 fluid oz) strained giblet stock, or water with 10g (⅓oz) dissolved beef stock cube
  6 juniper berries, crushed
  2 bay leaves, crumbled
  250ml (9 fluid oz) port
Finally add pheasant pieces. Cover and cook in 180C/350F oven 1¾ hours or until tender.
Stir in and reheat on stove with
  2 300g (11oz) tins haricot or butter beans, drained
Thicken as necessary with
  6-8 teaspoons cornflour, dissolved in equal quantity water
Now is the time either to place pastry crust in position on pie and return to oven 5-6 minutes for it to heat through, then serve. Or to refrigerate pie until required, reheat, and add pastry in the same way.
*For a cheaper dish, use chickens.

Good news for dieters—potatoes are not fattening! They are, in fact, a low-calorie high water-content food, no more fattening than apples.

Meat

Steak and Kidney Pudding, one of England's best known dishes, started off as Steak *or* Kidney Pudding. It often included at least a dozen oysters; but that was when they sold for four a penny, and housewives fattened them with oatmeal in the baby's bath!

To minimise work on the day, pudding can be prepared and steamed 3 hours the day before, steamed again 2 hours when required.

For suet pastry, combine in bowl
  150g (5oz) plain flour
  1 teaspoon baking powder
  ½ teaspoon salt
  150g (5oz) shredded suet mix
Add, to make a firm dough
  approx. 125ml (4½ fluid oz) cold water
Roll out ⅔ thinly, to fit 3 litre (5¼ pint) pudding basin. Roll out remainder and cut circle for lid, slightly larger than top of basin.
Grease basin and line with pastry.

Trim and cut into 2cm (¾") pieces
  8 lamb kidneys or 450g (1lb) ox kidney
  1¼kg (4lbs) chuck or similar stewing steak
Shake in plastic bag with
  150g (5oz) flour, seasoned with
  1 teaspoon salt and ⅛ teaspoon pepper
Discard excess flour. Put in basin. Add
  1 large onion, finely chopped
Pour on, up sides of basin
  approx. 375ml (13¾ fluid oz) stong beef stock, or water with 3 10g (⅓oz) dissolved stock cubes
Top with pastry lid, trimming edges just inside basin. Press to sides with fork, for airtight seal.
Cover top of basin with greased sheet of greaseproof paper, deeply pleated, and 2 sheets aluminium foil, pleated, to allow for expansion.
Stand pudding on plate in large saucepan with warm water ¾ up sides. Cover and simmer 5 hours, adding boiling water if necessary. Or cook over 2 days, as suggested above.
Serve in basin (in the old days this had a white napkin—probably double damask—around it) and pour in a little hot water at table, if more gravy is needed.

"Domestic occupations should never for one moment be neglected, as such neglect must produce misery and may, perhaps, ultimately terminate in *ruin*."
MODERN DOMESTIC COOKERY, 1835.

MIDDLE TEMPLE LANE, OFF FLEET STREET
Two barristers make their 20th century way in a world made familiar by the writings of Charles Dickens and Charles Lamb. Lit by gas lamps, it lies between Inner Temple and Middle Temple, two of the four great Inns of Court which hold the exclusive right to call people to the English Bar ... a statue nearby is inscribed 'Lawyers were children once.' According to Shakespeare's Henry VI, *the red and white roses worn as badges during the Wars of the Roses came from the Middle Temple Gardens.*

Only good wines should be used for cooking as it is the alcohol that evaporates, not the flavour.

Roast Beef and Yorkshire Pudding are as English as London itself. They are combined in this fascinating *Toad in a Hole* recipe from an 1838 cook book ... with a modern touch or two.

For pudding, combine until smooth—by hand in usual way, or in blender, with some liquid first to prevent clogging
  450ml (15 fluid oz) milk
  4 eggs
  225g (8oz) *self-raising* flour
  1 teaspoon salt
Put on one side. Melt in flameproof oven dish approx. 25cm (10") wide x 10cm (4") deep
  45g (1½oz) beef dripping or margarine
Swirl it around to coat sides. Remove from heat. Place in centre
  1½-1¾kg (3½-4lbs) roasting blade
    or similar beef
Pour batter around sides of beef. Cook uncovered in 180C/350F oven, allowing 25 minutes per 450g (lb). Remove meat to warmed platter to firm for carving. Serve pudding in dish with juices. If too fatty, pour them off, cover pudding to keep warm, and make Quick Gravy (Page 38).

Roast Lamb is equally English. But coffee, brandy and jelly replace the usual mint sauce.

Make slits with point of sharp knife in
  1¾-2¼kg (4-5lb) leg of lamb
Fill slits with
  2 large cloves garlic, slivered
Rub meat with
  1 teaspoon mustard powder, combined with
  3 teaspoons salt
Roast uncovered in 180C/350F oven, allowing 25 minutes per 450g (lb). 30 minutes before cooking is completed, heat in small pan
  1 cup strong fresh or instant coffee
  8 teaspoons red currant jelly
  6 teaspoons brandy
Pour over lamb. Finish cooking, basting once after 15 minutes. Let lamb rest on warmed dish to firm for carving, while thickening juices as required with
  3-4 teaspoons cornflour, dissolved in equal
    quantity water
Heat and stir until smooth. Pour a little over meat and serve rest separately.

Aluminium foil can be used many times if wiped clean and free of wrinkles with a damp cloth after use.

COVENT GARDEN

where Pygmalion's *Eliza Doolittle sold her flowers, was noted for its writers, actors and artists in the 19th century, and dates back to the 13th century convent garden owned by the monks of Westminster. Then came the Reformation. The monasteries were dissolved and the land reverted to the Crown. In 1552 it was a gift to the first earl of Bedford. In 1670 a licence was granted for a fruit and flower market to be established here and this became the largest and most famous in England. In 1974 it was moved to Nine Elms, near Vauxhall, and Covent Garden is now a tourist attraction.*

Pork with Dried Apricots. Combining meat with fruit is often thought to be an American invention. But such recipes appeared in *The Forme of Cury* (Manner of Cookery), one of the earliest existing records of English cooking, compiled in the late 1300s for Richard II.

Remove excess fat from
 1½kg (3½lbs) boneless shoulder blade pork
Cut into small dice and brown in batches in
 75ml (2½ fluid oz) oil
Transfer to large flameproof casserole.
Sauté until soft in pork pan
 2 medium onions, chopped
 200g (7oz) celery, chopped
Add to pork. Drain off any fat. Stir in
 750ml (1¼ pints) mild dry cider
Pour into casserole. Add
 200g (7oz) small carrots, cut into rounds
 175g (6oz) dried apricots, roughly chopped
 90g (3oz) seedless raisins
 4 teaspoons chopped parsley
 4 teaspoons lemon juice
 1 teaspoon each salt and brown sugar
 ½ teaspoon powdered ginger
 ½ teaspoon each dill seed and pepper
 ½ teaspoon fresh chopped thyme, or
  ¼ teaspoon dried
 ¼ teaspoon ground cloves
Stir to mix well. Cover. Cook in 180C/350F oven 2½ hours or until pork is tender.
Thicken sauce with
 6-8 teaspoons cornflour, dissolved in equal
  quantity water
Reheat, stirring, on stove. Serve, or refrigerate and reheat when required.

ROMAN WALL AT BARBICAN
Barbican means a projecting watch tower over the gate of a fortified town. The remains of this tower are part of the stone wall built around London by the Romans almost 2,000 years ago.

Boiled Leg of Lamb and Caper Sauce. A modern version of the boiled haunch of mutton with caper sauce that was a great favourite at public dinners in London in the 19th century.

Wash and remove excess fat from
  1¾-2¼kg (4-5lbs) leg of lamb
Cover with cold water in large saucepan. Add
  1 medium peeled whole onion
  1 small bunch parsley
  ½ teaspoon whole black peppercorns
  1½ teaspoons salt and a bouquet garni
Bring to boil. Spoon off any scum. Cover, reduce heat, and keep boiling gently 1¾-2 hours or until meat is tender.
If cooked ahead, cool in stock.
*When required, combine in small saucepan
  60g (2oz) flour, with
  60g (2oz) melted butter or margarine
Cook until bubbly. Remove from heat. Stir in
  150ml (5 fluid oz) strained lamb stock
  150ml (5 fluid oz) milk
  4 teaspoons dry sherry
Cook, stirring, over medium heat until thick. Let simmer on low heat 2-3 minutes. Stir in
  8 teaspoons drained capers, finely chopped
  4 teaspoons finely chopped parsley
  150ml (5 fluid oz) single cream
  1 teaspoon salt
  ⅛ teaspoon white pepper
Heat gently without boiling.
Remove meat from hot stock. Place on warm dish. Pour a little sauce over it, topped with sprig of parsley, and serve rest separately.

Boiled Beef and Carrots, an old cockney dish still celebrated in the music hall song of the same name.

Place in large pan
  2kg (4½lbs) salt/corned silverside,
    pre-soaked if necessary
  2 each carrots and onions, quartered
  8 teaspoons brown sugar
  6 peppercorns
Cover with water. Bring to boil. Remove any scum. Simmer, covered, 2-3 hours until tender. Cool in stock.
When required, remove meat and discard vegetables. Cook in stock required quantity of
  carrots, onions, potatoes or dumplings
When done, add beef, whole or sliced. Simmer until heated through.
Serve with pease pudding—traditional (Page 44), or avocado sauce—sensational (Page 48).

The brighter the colour of bottled herbs and spices, the better the flavour.

Oxtail Stew. Rich and delicious. The soup from which it is derived is said to have originated in 16th century Soho, when Huguenots escaping from France settled there among members of the Tanners' Guild. The tanners used to give them the tails left over from their ox hides.

A day ahead, remove any excess fat from
  1¾-2¼kg (4-5lbs) large lean oxtails, jointed
Shake all together in a plastic bag with
  90g (3oz) flour, seasoned with
  1½ teaspoons salt and ¼ teaspoon pepper
Discard excess flour and brown on all sides in heavy pan, a few at a time, in
  90g (3oz) dripping or margarine
Transfer, as they cook, with slotted spoon to large flameproof pan.
Quickly brown, adding fat if necessary
  3 large onions, sliced
Add to oxtail. Pour on
  750ml (1¼ pints) tin tomato juice
Add water to cover meat, with
  bouquet garni
  2 10g (⅓oz) beef stock cubes, crumbled
Bring to boil on stove. Cover. Cook in 150C/300F oven 4 hours, until meat is tender and almost falling off bones.
Remove bouquet garni. Cover and refrigerate.
*To serve, remove fat and reheat on stove. When beginning to boil, add as required
  celery, carrots, onions, thickly sliced
  medium potatoes, quartered, or dumplings
Boil gently until vegetables are cooked. Thicken sauce to taste with
  6-8 teaspoons cornflour, dissolved in equal quantity water
For special occasions add
  150ml (5 fluid oz) claret
Serve with bowls for the bones.

Suet Dumplings were a Norfolk speciality in the 18th and 19th centuries, and are referred to there as "20 minute swimmers"—simmered with stews, etc. for last 20 minutes of cooking time.

Combine
  110g (4oz) self-raising flour
  60g (2oz) shredded suet
  ⅛ teaspoon each salt and pepper
Add just enough cold water to make firm dough.
Divide into pieces and shape into balls with floured hands.

Good kitchen knives should never be washed in very hot water; it reduces their sharpness.

Lancashire Hot Pot. This recipe was made 100 or so years ago with mutton, 4 kidneys and 20 oysters, and cost about five shillings. Not cheap, when you consider the cook would have earned £15-£25 *a year*. Hot Pot, now, is usually served as a simple economical family dish so oysters and kidneys are omitted.

As mutton is virtually unobtainable, allowing 2 per person, remove superfluous fat from
  12-16 large best end neck of lamb chops
Place layer of chops in deep pan or casserole.
Top with layer taken from
  4-5 large onions, thinly sliced
  1⅓kg (3lbs) potatoes, thickly sliced
Sprinkle with
  ½ teaspoon each salt and mild curry powder
  ⅛ teaspoon pepper
Repeat, with solid layer potato on top.
Pour in
  450ml (15 fluid oz) beef stock, or water with
    2 10g (⅓oz) dissolved stock cubes
Cook covered in 180C/350F oven 2 hours.
Dot potatoes with
  a little butter or margarine
Cook uncovered further 30 minutes to brown.
*Hot Pot is normally served from pan with its own thin gravy. But it can be poured off and thickened with cornflour, if you wish.

Liver and Bacon Casserole.

Dip in seasoned flour
  900g (2lbs) calf or lamb liver, trimmed and cut
    into ¾cm (¼") thick slices
Sauté on both sides in
  90g (3oz) unsalted butter or margarine
Set aside. Sauté until soft
  225g (8oz) bacon, rind removed and chopped
  2 medium onions, sliced
In casserole, arrange layers of liver, bacon and onions. Top with
  425g (15oz) tin peeled tomatoes, chopped
  10g (⅓oz) beef stock cube, crumbled in
    juice from tin and water to half fill dish
  1 teaspoon salt and ¼ teaspoon pepper
Cover and cook in 180C/350F oven 1-1½ hours or until liver is tender.
Traditionally served with
  mashed swedes and pickled walnuts
*Leftovers, drained, become a tasty pâté in blender or processor.

GUILDHALL
Centre of government of the square mile that is the City of London for over 1,000 years. And, in spite of destruction by fire in 1666 and air raids in 1940, its oldest and probably its finest building. The Court of Common Council, its members the Lord Mayor, 25 Aldermen and 159 Common Councilmen, meets here and acts as local authority. It also maintains ancient ceremonies and traditions, details of which are available from the Information Centre at Guildhall. The annual procession of each new Lord Mayor dates back to the Charter of King John in 1215.

HORSE GUARDS AND ST. JAMES'S PARK GATES
Behind the stone building that succeeded the Whitehall Palace guard house, the Horse Guards Parade is used for ceremonies that include Trooping the Colour on the Queen's official birthday in June.
St. James's Park was laid out by order of Henry VIII and frequented by "sovereigns and ministers, courtiers and fops, lords and ladies, philosophers and thinkers." Charles I walked here on the way to his execution and, "by the pond that then was a favourite resort for intending suicides," Charles II dallied with his mistresses and played with his dogs. Some of the trees around it (a lake now) date back to the Restoration, when Charles returned to England in 1660 and was proclaimed king.

SOHO SQUARE
One of London's lovely surprises, a peaceful village green in an area teaming with multi-cultural restaurants and strip joints. It was laid out in 1681 on the site of a house belonging to the Duke of Monmouth, natural son of Charles II (whose statue stands in the Square), who fought to inherit the throne, was made king of Taunton, but ended up beheaded on Tower Hill. What looks like an historic hunting lodge is, sadly, an 1890 electricity substation!

Vegetables

High-rise does not just mean buildings these days; we also have to cope with ever increasing food prices. But this isn't all bad, as it has taught us to be imaginative when we prepare our meals. With meat and fish, for instance, we are learning to allow smaller portions and to pay more attention to the vegetables we serve with them, or as a substitute for them.

Cauliflower Curry makes an interesting change from the familiar Cauliflower Cheese. Paired with boiled rice, pappadams and chutney, it's a meal in itself.

In large saucepan, heat
  90ml (3 fluid oz) oil
Stir in
  600g (1¼lbs) onions, cut into cubes
  5 cloves garlic, finely chopped or crushed
  8 teaspoons finely chopped fresh ginger
  2 teaspoons ground coriander
  2 teaspoons ground cumin
  6 teaspoons ground turmeric
  1 teaspoon each chilli powder and pepper
Cook, stirring occasionally, until onions are soft.
Stir in
  ½ large cauliflower, cut into small chunks
  800g (1¾lbs) unpeeled potatoes, cut into cubes
Mix until coated with spice mixture. Add
  3 425g (15oz) tins peeled tomatoes and juice
  375ml (13 fluid oz) water
Simmer gently, covered, about ¾ hour or until potatoes are cooked but still firm.
Just before serving, stir in
  30g (1oz) desiccated coconut
  60g (2oz) cashews or skinned almonds.
  175g (6oz) sultanas

"There is in every cook's opinion,
No savoury dish without an onion:
But lest your kissing should be spoiled
The onion must be thoroughly boiled."
DEAN JONATHAN SWIFT, 1667-1745.

The eggplant was introduced into England in 1587. Called *mala insana* (mad apple) it was, in fact, believed to cause madness if eaten, and grown only as an ornamental plant for several hundred years.

Frozen Vegetables, for cooks in a hurry, do well with a few extra touches.

Cauliflower. Cook large pack as directed. Serve topped with sauce made from small pack frozen peas, cooked at same time, then mashed in blender or processor with cream and seasoning.

Spinach. Cook and drain. Add salt, with a little butter, cream, and grated nutmeg.

Brussels Sprouts. Cook until tender but still firm. Season, and toss with chopped walnuts heated in melted butter.

Pease Pudding used to mean boiling split peas in a cloth 2½ hours, sieving them, beating them 10 minutes, and boiling them another 2 hours. No more: this recipe from a clever friend is so easy, I wonder why I never thought of it.

Cook briefly as packet instructions
  100g quick-dried peas, with
  sugar and salt
Drain. Combine in blender or processor with
  ½-¾ metric (tea) cup warm milk
until smooth and consistency of mashed potato. Add extra seasoning if required, and serve immediately in warmed bowl. Or keep hot for a short time in a low oven or over hot water.
*Traditionally served with boiled beef or pork, but a good side dish at any time.

Mange-tout, Sugar or Snow Peas are eaten pod and all with minimum cooking. Peas are so ancient, their origins are unknown. The oldest find so far was on the border between Burma and Thailand, carbon-dated at 9750 BC.

Simply steam over boiling water 1 minute
  500g (18oz) sugar peas, topped, tailed, and with strings removed
Put into warm serving dish. Stir in lightly
  45g (1½oz) butter or margarine
  salt and pepper to taste
Serve immediately.

Soured red wine, no longer fit to drink, makes an excellent vinegar.

THE OLD BAILEY, OR CENTRAL CRIMINAL COURT
built on the site of the old, infamous Newgate Prison and scene of most of England's famous trials of murderers and spies. A popular place when hangings were carried out in public and rooms in nearby pubs were rented for a good view and a happy day's outing. A convenient place, wrote Henry Mayhew in 1881: "You can be tried there, sentenced there, condemn-celled there, and comfortably hanged and buried there, without having to leave the building, except for the purpose of going to the scaffold."

PROSPECT OF WHITBY AT ST. KATHERINE'S DOCK
First built in 1520 and one of London's oldest public houses, it was known as the Devil's Tavern because of its involvement with smugglers and pirates ... Captain Kidd was hanged nearby. 'Bloody' Judge Jeffreys watched river executions here, Whistler and Turner painted from the balcony, and Pepys was a constant visitor.
Pubs replaced taverns, where drinks only were served, and inns which offered food, lodging, and ale that was often brewed by churches to raise funds. Guests slept in dormitories, and records show charges of a halfpenny for a bed, a farthing for soup.

Colcannon will not create a sensation. But it is a pleasant traditional dish that combines a cooked vegetable—usually cabbage, with mashed potato. It is often confused with bubble and squeak but this, originally, was a mixture of cabbage and boiled beef.

Boil separately in large saucepans
  700g (1½lbs) potatoes, quartered
  700g (1½lbs) young cabbage, shredded
Drain well. Mash potatoes in saucepan with
  milk from 110ml (4 fluid oz), to make firm
    creamy mixture
Stir in cabbage, over medium heat, with
  6 spring onions/shallots, chopped—saving
    a few for garnish
  60g (2oz) butter or margarine
  salt and white pepper to taste
Serve very hot, piled on heated dish.
Or press into greased oven dish and top with
  generous dabs butter or margarine
When required, cook in 180C/350F oven 30 minutes or until well heated through.
Either way, garnish with reserved onions.

Sauces

When it comes to minimum effort maximum effect, sauces probably top the list. They make the simplest food instantly special.

Anchovy Sauce, for instance, transforms a plain lettuce and tomato salad, adds flavour and interest to grilled steaks or quickly fried veal escalopes.

Stir on low heat in small saucepan
200g (7oz) unsalted butter, melted, with
30 flat anchovies (3 small tins) drained on paper towelling and finely chopped
(for less salty sauce, soak them briefly in water before draining and chopping)
4 teaspoons lemon juice
½ teaspoon paprika
Simmer, stirring, 3-4 minutes or until anchovies have dissolved. Pour hot over salad or meat, or refrigerate and reheat when required.

Garlic Sauce is even more versatile. Superb hot with fish, roast beef or poultry. Cold, as dressing for potato salad, topping for open meat sandwiches, even as a dip with chilled vegetable pieces.

Bring to boil
375ml (13 fluid oz) chicken stock, or water with 10g (⅓oz) dissolved stock cube
Stir in
6 cloves garlic, crushed
90g (3oz) ground almonds
30g (1oz) day-old crustless bread, crumbled
Simmer and stir continuously 5 minutes, until bread lumps have dissolved.
Serve. Or reheat when required. Or chill.

"In general, mankind, since the improvement of cookery, eats about twice as much as nature requires... Nothing is more common in the newspapers, than instances of people who, after eating a hearty supper, are found dead in bed in the morning."
THE YOUNG WOMAN'S COMPANION: OR FRUGAL HOUSEWIFE (ANONYMOUS), 1811.

Poor Man's Sauce, from an 1822 cook book. It was, wrote the author, "in much esteem in France, where people of taste, weary of rich dishes, to obtain the charm of variety, occasionally order the fare of the peasant."

Stir together in sauce-boat or jug
1 metric (tea) cup chopped parsley
10 spring onions/shallots, finely chopped
110ml (4 fluid oz) oil
200ml (7 fluid oz) vinegar
salt and black pepper to taste
a finely chopped pickled gherkin, or
a little grated horseradish (optional).

Quick Gravy.

In saucepan, sauté until soft
2 spring onions/shallots, chopped, in
30g (1oz) butter or margarine
Stir in
450ml (15 fluid oz) beef stock, or water with
10g (⅓oz) dissolved stock cube
Season to taste with
dry sherry or Worcestershire sauce
salt and pepper
Thicken as required with
3-4 teaspoons cornflour, dissolved in
equal quantity of water
*For an especially good gravy at a moment's notice, save juices each time meat and poultry are roasted. Refrigerate them, remove fat when set, and freeze in separate batches, to add to this recipe before seasoning and thickening.

Avocado Sauce adds glamour to boiled beef, which normally isn't glamorous at all.

Mash in blender or processor
2 ripe avocado pears
Add to them, according to their size
¼-½ metric (tea) cup sour cream
1-2 teaspoons lemon juice
⅛-¼ teaspoon seasoned salt
light sprinkle white pepper
light sprinkle garlic powder (optional)
*I make a point of buying pears reduced in price because of a few brown spots that are easily removed.

Salad dressings were unknown in England, until introduced by French refugees from the Revolution.

After the Main Course

"As every one's attention should be entirely given up to what is on the table, and not to what surrounds *it—ladies should not expect particular notice until the dessert is served. The sex then recovers all its rights, and its empire is never less disputed."*

ESSAYS, MORAL, PHILOSOPHICAL, AND STOMACHICAL on the Important Science of Good-Living, by Launcelot Sturgeon, Esq., and dedicated to the Right Worshipful the Court of Aldermen of the City of London, 1822.

Desserts

I can never understand why so many clever and creative cooks will take infinite pains to produce a superb meal and then spoil the whole effect with a bought dessert because, they say, it is too hard or too time consuming to make one. But it isn't. Even for cooks who are not creative and clever. It is all a matter of using the right recipes.

Syllabub. The Royal London Syllabub of some 200 years ago was a sweet—and powerful! —liquid made by milking a cow into a bowl of Madeira, port, sherry, brandy, sugar and nutmeg. Today we are more familiar with adaptations of a later 'solid' syllabub.

In chilled bowl, combine and beat until thick
  450ml (15 fluid oz) chilled double cream
  90ml (3 fluid oz) sherry
  45ml (1½ fluid oz) brandy
  75g (2½oz) caster sugar
  juice of half a lemon
  a little grated nutmeg
Pile into glasses and chill.

Fruit Fantasy. A splendid sweet sent to me by a reader. I am very grateful.

Well ahead of time, combine in large bowl
  approx. 90g (3oz) packet strawberry jelly
  110ml (4 fluid oz) boiling water
Stir until fully dissolved. Then fold in
  450g (1lb) tin crushed pineapple, drained
  2 small bananas, mashed
  60g (2oz) walnuts, roughly chopped
Add gently, to keep their shape
  225g (8oz) stawberries, washed, hulled,
    and sliced
Spoon half of mixture into 20cm (8") shallow flan or pie dish. Refrigerate until firm.
Then cover with
  300g (10oz) sour cream, softened with
  3 teaspoons kirsch or leftover pineapple juice
Top with remaining unset mixture. Refrigerate again to set. Slice and serve with
  whipped cream
on the side for those who want it.

Unusual Easy Cherry Ice Cream.

Combine in bowl
  425g (15oz) tin pitted dark cherries in syrup, drained and roughly chopped
  175g (6oz) caster sugar
Leave 30 minutes, while pre-setting freezer to its lowest, and chilling mixing bowl, beater, ice cream container, and
  300ml (10 fluid oz) carton double cream
Beat cream until thick but not stiff. Drain any accumulated juice from cherries and gently stir them into cream. Freeze, covered, in container 3 hours or until firm. Transfer to refrigerator 30 minutes before serving.
Decorate, if you wish, with additional cherries.

Boodle's Orange Fool is a legacy from the days when London Clubs provided a forum for men of widely differing views. Boodle's, London's second oldest Club (after Whites'), opened in 1762 and was primarily political, strongly Whig.

The recipe is not a true fool—which does not include cake; slightly resembles trifle—which does. You may care to increase the resemblance with a little liquor.

Ahead of time, arrange in attractive serving bowl
  4-6 small sponge cakes, quartered, or a large sponge, sliced
Juice in a mixing bowl
  4 large oranges and 2 lemons
Stir in
  grated rind from 2 oranges and 1 lemon
  60ml (2 fluid oz) Marsala or sherry (optional)
  600ml (1 pint) single cream
  caster sugar to taste
Pour over cake. Allow to stand 2-3 hours.
It looks best topped before serving with whipped cream.

"Among certain of the higher and more opulent classes of society, where great style is affected, it is not unusual to present dinners consisting of ... 1st, a course of soups; 2d, fish; 3d, meat and poultry; 4th, puddings, tarts, blamanges (sic), jellies, and game; 5th, cheese; and then the dessert (fresh and crystallized fruits, cakes, biscuits, ices, nuts) and dessert wine."
CHAMBERS COOKERY FOR YOUNG HOUSEWIVES, 1838.

THE WIG AND PEN CLUB AT Nos. 229-230 STRAND
No. 229 is the oldest building in the Strand. Built in 1625 on Roman ruins, it survived the Great Fire of London, and its stairway is the only one of its kind left in the world.
In Jacobean times, the house (its timber frame now hidden by plaster) was occupied by the gatekeeper for Temple Bar, which marked the boundary between the City of London and Westminster. Its first recorded use as an eating house was when "a penn'orth of meat and bread" was served to crowds gathered outside to view the heads of traitors and criminals spiked on the gateway. A Victorian monument has replaced this, but the Queen still stops here for ritual permission to enter the City.

Peeres in Comfit. A modern version of a 14th century dish, it smells and tastes wonderful.

Drain on paper towelling, allowing 2 per person
  12-16 tinned pear halves
Combine in large shallow pan
  350ml (12 fluid oz) marsala, or other sweet heavy wine
  125g (4½oz) caster sugar
  1¼ teaspoons very fresh ground ginger
Stir until boiling. Simmer 4-5 minutes, until slightly reduced and thickened. Add pears, core-side-down. Baste with syrup. Reheat and simmer a few minutes.
Serve warm or cold.

Ricotta Cream. After a rich main course, this low-fat substitute for cream, to serve with pudding, can be very welcome.

Simply combine in blender at high speed
  150g (5oz) very fresh Ricotta cheese
  45ml (1½oz) liquid skim milk, followed by lemon juice and sugar to taste.

ST. ETHELDREDA'S AT ELY PLACE
Interior of the first pre-Reformation shrine returned to the Catholics in England and Wales. Built c. 1290, it is all that is left of a vast complex of buildings occupied or visited by Kings, Queens, Ambassadors, Statesmen and Prelates, and which included Ely House where John of Gaunt died in 1399.

Apple Charlotte. The first of its kind is said to have been created in the royal kitchens of George III (whose policies lost England her American colonies) and named for his wife, Charlotte Sophia. Traditionally made as a bread-and-butter mould, with fruit in the middle. I prefer this lighter variation, with the bread crumbled and fried in the butter.

Fry until crisp, carefully stirring and turning to prevent burning
  225g (8oz) white breadcrumbs, quickly made in processor or blender, in
  90g (3oz) unsalted butter, melted
Mash
  2 411g (14½oz) tins unsweetened pie apples, with
  110g (4oz) brown sugar mixed with
  4 teaspoons lemon juice
  ½ teaspoon cinnamon
Arrange layers of apple and fried crumbs in glass bowl, with crumbs on top. Chill.
To serve, I break with tradition even further and cover Charlotte with
  whipped cream, sprinkled with
  chocolate shaved into curls with potato peeler.

Iced Cheese Savoury makes a fascinating change from the usual sweet course. Or can follow it. In fact, savouries were invented, in Queen Victoria's day, to cleanse the palate after the sweet and prepare it for the cheese and dessert to follow (see Page 52).

Beat until soft in warmed bowl
  110g (4oz) butter or margarine
Add and beat until combined and smooth
  100g (3½oz) Roquefort or other blue-vein cheese, chopped
  110ml (4 fluid oz) single cream
  ¾ teaspoon paprika
Stir in
  4-6 teaspoons finely chopped spring onions/shallots
Pack into lightly oiled (spray is best) ice cream tray and freeze 1 hour. Turn out and refrigerate in plastic bag.
When required, turn upside-down on lettuce leaves. Pattern lightly with fork. Slice at table and serve on small plates with
  chilled lettuce-heart leaves
  hot dry toast or water biscuits.

NASH TERRACES AT REGENT'S PARK
A magnificent legacy from architect John Nash, who redesigned Henry VIII's royal hunting ground, Marylebone Park, as an elegant garden suburb renamed in honour of George Augustus Frederick, who became Prince regent in 1811 when George III, his father, was certified permanently deranged. He is remembered more for his tempestuous liaison with Mrs. Fitzherbert and their illegal marriage than for the Catholic Emancipation Act that was passed in 1829, during his reign as George IV.

There must be hundreds of recipes for baked, boiled and steamed puddings, many of them named for the areas where they originated. Some are basic and boring and unbelievably stodgy (the first one I made was so heavy, the doctor thought I had appendicitis!), while others are exceptionally good.

Baked Date and Walnut Pudding is one of my favourites. It's rich, but it still manages to be light and spongy.

In large bowl cream together
  250g (9oz) butter or margarine, melted
  110g (4oz) brown sugar
Stir in and mix well
  3 eggs, lightly beaten
  90ml (3 fluid oz) milk
  110g (4oz) self-raising flour
  ½ teaspoon vanilla essence
Add and stir until well mixed through
  110g (4oz) walnut pieces
  110g (4oz) stoned dates, chopped
Pour into greased oven-to-table dish. Cook, uncovered, in 200C/400F oven 1-1¼ hours or until knife in centre comes out clean.
Serve hot with
  liquid or whipped cream.

Steamed Dried Fig Pudding is another favourite. Light textured, with a delicate flavour, and particularly easy to make.

Simply combine in mixing bowl
  375g (13oz) dried figs, stalks removed and finely chopped
  250g (9oz) prepared suet mix
  2 eggs, well beaten
  65g (2¼oz) seedless raisins
  60ml (2 fluid oz) milk
  60ml (2 fluid oz) port
  125g (4½oz) sugar
  90g (3oz) self-raising flour
  ¼ teaspoon salt
Mix thoroughly. Put into well-greased pudding basin. Cover top securely with double layer aluminium foil, greased and pleated for expansion. Place in large saucepan on upturned saucer, with hot water ½ way up sides. Cover and steam on gentle boil, adding water if necessary, 4 hours or until knife in centre comes out clean. Unmoulding can be a problem, so serve in basin with
  custard or cream.

HYDE PARK

was once a dense forest, home of wild boars and bulls. Owned by the monks of Westminster for centuries, Henry VIII enclosed it as a royal chase when the Abbey was dissolved, filling it with deer. It was opened to the public by James I, but it was not until the reign of Charles II that it became a lively venue for foot and horse racing, morris dances, and hurling—a mixture of football and wrestling; a place where lords and ladies promenaded in their best finery, hoping to be noticed by the king.

To win a wager in 1766, a man crossed the Thames on a butcher's tray with only his hands for paddles.

Summer Pudding was sometimes disconcertingly called Hydropathic Pudding because of its popularity at health resorts where rich food was forbidden. At its delicious best with fresh summer fruit—berries, cherries, currants—but tinned fruit can also be used so as to enjoy it all year round.

Line bottom and sides of 1½ litre (2½ pint) pudding basin with

approx. 8 thin slices day-old crustless milk bread, saving 3-4 more slices for top

Make sure there are no gaps. Drain, saving juice, enough fruit to fill basin from

1 425g (15oz) tin each strawberries, raspberries, blackberries, pitted cherries

Top with

60-90g (2-3oz) caster sugar, to taste
150ml (5 fluid oz) fruit juice

Cover well with remaining bread, cut to shape. Put plate on top, weighed down with 1-2 heavy tins, and refrigerate overnight.
To unmould, run knife between pudding and basin, cover with serving plate, and turn over quickly ... don't worry if it sags a little. Use remaining juice to colour any white patches.
Serve with plenty of

liquid or whipped cream

*900g (2lbs) fresh fruit is simmered 2-3 minutes with 175g (6oz) sugar to create juice.

Port Wine Jelly, an education for people who thought jellies were just for kids! In medieval times, they were extraordinarily elaborate: shaped like castles and decorated with liquid gold.

Dissolve as packet instructions

30g (3 envelopes) unflavoured gelatine, in
250ml (9 fluid oz) hot water

Stir in until completely dissolved

110g (4oz) caster sugar

Add

750ml (1¼ pints) good quality port
8 teaspoons strained lemon juice

Pour into attractive glass serving dish and refrigerate at least 5 hours or until set.
Serve with

whipped cream, to soften the strong alcohol flavour, and
fresh, stewed or preserved fruit.

Simple Lemon Meringue Pie.

Line 20cm (8") shallow pie dish, as packet instructions, with

ready-made shortcrust pastry

Bake as directed. Leave to cool.

In mixing bowl, beat on low speed until blended

425g (15oz) tin sweetened condensed milk
2 egg yolks, saving whites for meringue
125ml (4½oz) lemon juice
a little grated lemon rind
⅛ teaspoon salt

Fill pie shell. Beat until fairly stiff

2 reserved egg whites, with
¼ teaspoon cream of tartar

Add gradually

90g (3oz) caster sugar

Beat until smooth and standing in stiff peaks when beater is lifted. Cover filling and pastry completely. Bake in 220C/425F oven 5-8 minutes or until meringue is lightly browned.

Serve cold, but not chilled in refrigerator.

And to serve with after-dinner tea or coffee ...

Apricot and Coconut Balls.

For approx. 48 tiny balls, 24 larger ones, mix with spoon in bowl well ahead of time

225g (8oz) dried apricots, ready minced or chopped in blender
60g (2oz) brown sugar
60g (2oz) desiccated coconut
½ 425g (15oz) tin sweetened condensed milk

Leave an hour or so to firm. Form into balls, scooping mixture out with small spoon for even sizes. Roll in desiccated coconut.

Store in sealed container in refrigerator or freezer until serving.

Tea and Coffee

Tea and coffee are such an everyday part of our everyday lives, it is quite startling to discover how comparatively recent this is.

London's first coffee house did not open until 1652, although others followed at a great rate. They came to be known as 'penny universities,' because men of every occupation and political persuasion met there to discuss affairs of the day, and the entrance fee was a penny.

It was not for another century, some 200 years ago, that tea came into its own. This was when the coffee houses began to lose favour, closing down or becoming private clubs or chop houses, and the London tea gardens took their place. They offered walks and fireworks, promenade concerts, bowling greens and rooms for dancing, and it was here that tea was served in public to *both sexes* for the very first time.

The life of the coffee houses was brief but it was never dull. And not just in England. In Turkey, the Grand Vizier considered them hotbeds of sedition and ordered them closed; first offenders were beaten, second offenders sewn into leather bags and thrown in the Bosporus. Charles II also feared them as centres of political intrigue and issued a proclamation for their suppression in 1675, but there was such a public outcry he had to cancel it eleven days later.

Both tea and coffee were violently opposed as health hazards. Coffee, it was said, produced languor and paralysis. While tea caused weakness of the nerves, flabbiness of the flesh, and a pale wan complexion!

How marvellous that we can disregard such awful warnings. That we can fearlessly enjoy the special cup of tea or coffee which adds the perfect finishing touch to a special meal ... however we serve it.

Flaming Coffee is audience-participation coffee, which makes it ideal for parties.
Pass small cups of freshly brewed coffee with teaspoons, a bowl of sugar cubes, a bottle of cognac or rum—and a box of matches. Guests put a sugar cube in their spoon, pour liquor over it, warm it with a lighted match under the spoon, set it alight and, when the flames die down, stir it into their coffee.

Cinnamon Tea is an ideal after-dinner tea.
Make a pot of tea as usual and add a 7½cm (3") cinnamon stick. Allow to brew. Pour and add 2-3 teaspoons Grand Marnier, to each guest's taste. And pass the sugar.

Index

Before the Main Course

Cheddar Cheese Dip 13
Prawns in Bacon 13

A Most Unusual Chilled Walnut Soup 17
Baked Soup 17
Cock-a-leekie 18
Creamy Chilled Mushroom Soup 16
Mulligatawny Soup 15
Stilton Soup 16
Superb Devonshire Cauliflower Soup 18

Cool Minted Pears 19
Hot Fish Mousse 19
Spinach and Ricotta Pie 20

Remarkable Wholemeal Bread 20

The Main Course

Fish with Mayonnaise and Bread Cubes 26
Savoury Salmon Custard 23
Simple Spicy Special Kedgeree 23
Sweet and Sour Fish Fillets with Ginger 26

Chicken with Seafood Sauce 27
Chicken Baked with Curry Sauce 28
Chicken Ring 28

Pheasant Pie 30

Boiled Beef and Carrots 36
Boiled Leg of Lamb and Caper Sauce 36
Lancashire Hot Pot 38
Liver and Bacon Casserole 38
Oxtail Stew 37
Pork with Dried Apricots 35
Roast Beef and Yorkshire Pudding
(Toad in a Hole) 33
Roast Lamb with Coffee and Brandy Sauce .. 33
Steak and Kidney Pudding 31
Suet Dumplings 37

Cauliflower Curry 43
Colcannon 46
Frozen Vegetables 44
Mange-tout, Sugar or Snow Peas 44
Pease Pudding 44

Anchovy Sauce 47
Avocado Sauce 48
Garlic Sauce 47
Poor Man's Sauce 48
Quick Gravy 48

After the Main Course

Apple Charlotte 55
Baked Date and Walnut Pudding 58
Boodle's Orange Fool 52
Fruit Fantasy 51
Iced Cheese Savoury 55
Peeres in Comfit 54
Port Wine Jelly 60
Ricotta Cream 54
Simple Lemon Meringue Pie 61
Steamed Dried Fig Pudding 58
Summer Pudding 60
Syllabub 51
Unusual Easy Cherry Ice Cream 52

Apricot and Coconut Balls 61

Cinnamon Tea 62
Flaming Coffee 62